Help Me Be Good

Bullying

Joy Berry
Illustrated by Bartholomew

Joy Berry Books
New York

This book is about Sam and Brad.

Reading about Sam and Brad can help you understand and deal with being bullied.

Bullies are people who act tough and like to fight.

Bullies like to frighten or hurt people who are smaller or weaker than they are.

Some people become bullies because they feel inferior. They feel that they are not as good as other people.

Bullies act tough and fight so they can feel that they are as good as or better than other people.

Some people become bullies because they need attention. They want people to notice them.

Bullies act tough and fight so people will notice them.

Some people become bullies because they are frightened. They are afraid other people might hurt them.

Bullies act tough so people will fear them and not bother them.

Some people become bullies because they are angry. They want to show their anger when something upsets them.

Bullies express anger by being mean and fighting with other people.

You are being bullied when someone tries
to control you or tries to frighten you into
doing something.

Being bullied can upset you. It can make you angry.

There are things you can do to avoid being bullied.

Treat bullies the same way you treat other people.
Be kind to them.

Even bullies find it hard to be mean to a kind person.

Sometimes kindness does not stop bullies.

Stay away from bullies if being kind to them does not help.

Bullies cannot bother you if you are not around them.

Ignore bullies if you have to be around them. Do not look at them. Do not listen to them. Do not respond to them.

Bullies are less likely to bother you if you do not pay attention to them.

Confront bullies if it is impossible to ignore them.

Face them. Look into their eyes. Tell them you do not want to be bullied. Tell them to leave you alone.

Walk or run away from bullies if they insist on fighting.

Bullies cannot fight with you if you are not around.

Get help if bullies keep bothering you.

Talk to your parents, teacher, or babysitter. Ask for help in handling bullies who are bothering you.

No one likes to be bullied. You can avoid being bullied by handling bullies the right way. It is up to you.

Joy Berry Enterprises
146 West 29th St., Suite 11RW
New York, NY 10001

Cover Design & Art Direction: John Bellaud
Cover Illustration & Art Production: Geoff Glisson

Production Location: HX Printing, Guangzhou, China
Date of Production: July 2010
Cohort: Batch 1

Printed in China
ISBN 978-1-60577-140-3